T0011063

THE LITTLE GUIDE TO

LOUIS VUITTON

Published in 2023 by OH!
An Imprint of Welbeck Non-Fiction Limited,
part of Welbeck Publishing Group.
Offices in London – 20 Mortimer Street, London W1T 3JW
and Sydney – Level 17, 207 Kent St, Sydney NSW 2000 Australia
www.welbeckpublishing.com

ISBN 978-1-80069-533-7

Compiled and written by: David Clayton
Editorial: Victoria Denne
Project manager: Russell Porter
Production: Jess Brisley

A CIP catalogue record for this book is available from the British Library

Printed in China

10 9 8 7 6 5 4 3 2 1

THE LITTLE GUIDE TO

LOUIS VUITTON

STYLE TO LIVE BY
Unofficial and Unauthorized

CONTENTS

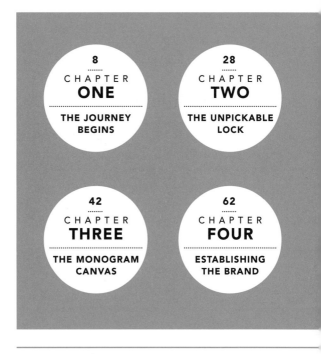

INTRODUCTION

The mere mention of Louis Vuitton evokes thoughts of luxury, elegance and timeless style. The French designer was a visionary pioneer, and the story of his iconic brand – from its humble beginnings to the global powerhouse that it is today – is a remarkable one that spans generations.

Hailing from the Jura region of eastern France, Louis was orphaned at the age of 10. At 13, he left home on foot to find his fortune in Paris. Working odd jobs along the way, he reached the city in 1837, where he became an apprentice to respected trunk maker Monsieur Maréchal. He quickly excelled, earning a reputation for an impeccable attention to detail – a quality that would set him apart from his contemporaries.

In 1854, Louis finally branched out on his own and opened his first packaging and trunk-making service in Paris. His name soon became associated with innovation and luxury, and his products were highly sought after. As the brand continued to grow, the designer's son, Georges Ferréol Vuitton, took over the running of the company, introducing the iconic Monogram Canvas that established the Vuitton brand and feel that remains to this day.

Revitalized, and now a global brand, Louis Vuitton would eventually launch into fashion and establish itself as a leader in luxury goods in Europe, producing high-end handbags, wallets and purses.

Passed through the generations from father to son, and overseen by iconic designers such as Marc Jacobs, Virgil Abloh and the newly appointed Pharrell Williams, the brand has continued to thrive. From the impeccable craftsmanship of its iconic trunks to the ever-evolving collections that push the boundaries of style, the fashion house has retained its edge without losing its classic appeal.

Whether you are a fashion enthusiast, a collector or simply intrigued by the world of luxury, this book will take you on a delightful journey into the captivating world of Louis Vuitton. Packed full of fascinating facts and carefully curated quotes, it's a rich celebration of the brand that forever changed fashion history.

CHAPTER
ONE

THE JOURNEY BEGINS

LOUIS VUITTON'S AMBITION
COULD ONLY BE SATISFIED
BY LEAVING HIS HUMBLE LIFE IN
EASTERN FRANCE AND SETTING
OUT TO FIND HIS FORTUNE
IN PARIS. THE 13-YEAR-OLD
MADE THE JOURNEY ON FOOT,
A DISTANCE OF ALMOST
300 MILES...

Louis Vuitton was born on 4 August 1821, in Anchay, a small working-class village in the east of France. His father, Xavier Vuitton, was a farmer and his mother, Coronne Gaillard – who died when he was 10 – a miller and part-time hat-maker.

The Vuitton family were a mix of carpenters, artisans and farmers, all good with their hands in one form or another, and Louis quickly learned skills from those around him.

But he also had a naturally artistic eye that set him apart from his contemporaries.

After tragically losing both parents and failing to settle with his adoptive family, Louis left home and between the ages of 13 and 15 steadily made his way to Paris from his home in the Jura department of eastern France. He took odd jobs, many with craftsmen and artisans, to pay for food and took shelter where and when he could find it, all the while improving his embryonic craft.

Louis had learned from a number of craftsmen and artisans along his journey, and upon arrival in Paris in 1837, he became an apprentice to the highly respected box-maker and packer Monsieur Maréchal.

Louis impressed Maréchal with the skills he had already learned and, under the watchful eye of his meticulous and highly skilled employer, honed his style and remained in situ for the next 17 years, gaining a reputation as one of the best in his field in the French capital.

Maréchal's workshop on Rue Saint-Honoré was a stone's throw from the luxurious shops and boulevards of the glamorous centre of Paris – something that beguiled Louis, who was inspired by the fashionable displays they presented and their sophisticated clientele.

Louis Vuitton's reputation was further enhanced when, in 1853, he was appointed the personal box-maker and packer of the Empress of France, Eugenie de Montijo – the wife of Napoleon III.

The Empress de Montijo charged Vuitton with beautifully packaging her clothes for transportation between the Tuileres Palace, the Château de Saint-Cloud and various seaside resorts.

In turn, this opened up a whole new world for Vuitton, who quickly became in demand to a new class of elite and royal clientele.

On 22 April 1854, Louis Vuitton married mill owner's daughter Clémence-Émilie Parriaux. He was 33 and she was 16.

In the same year, Louis founded a workshop of his own at 4 Rue Neuvedes-Capucines, close to the Place Vendôme, specializing in packing high-fashion and fragile items.

Vuitton's popularity among the aristocracy quicky grew. His ability to create stylish yet lightweight poplar-wood trunks further enhanced his position in what was then a niche market.

> **"**
>
> Securely packs the most fragile objects. Specializing in packing fashions.
>
> **"**

The sign outside Louis Vuitton's first shop, opened in Paris in 1854

"

The Louis Vuitton trunk is one of the most iconic luggage pieces in fashion history. There are many elements to the Louis Vuitton trunk which have been meticulously designed. From structure to hardware and leather to monogram, each element has a rich history.

"

As quoted on TheRestory.com's feature on "The History of the Louis Vuitton Trunk"

Vuitton's simple tweak on trunk designs of the day – a flat lid rather than a rounded one – proved a huge success as rail and boat travel were booming, but it also left him open to imitators.

Patent laws were easy to bypass or find loopholes in and other manufacturers quickly imitated Vuitton's work. His response was to add beechwood slats that became unique to his trunks.

In 1857, three years after they married, Louis and Clémence-Émilie had their first and only child, Georges Ferréol Vuitton, who would become the heir to the future global empire his father was creating.

By 1859, business was so good he had to relocate his workshop to bigger premises just outside Paris.

66

The early success of Louis Vuitton meant he had to expand his operations. This led to the 1859 opening of his atelier in Asnières. Just northeast of the centre of Paris, the workshop started with 20 employees. In 1900, there were nearly 100 people and by 1914 there were 225.

99

As quoted on LouisVuitton.com's "A Legendary History"

In 1867 Vuitton was awarded a bronze medal at the Exposition Universelle, an international exposition organized by Napoleon and held in Paris, which further enhanced his reputation for exceptional products and increased the demand for his goods.

The outbreak of the Franco-Prussian War in 1870 would almost certainly have ruined the business of a lesser mortal, with Vuitton's premises ransacked, tools and equipment stolen, and staff gone.

Instead, within six months, he had relocated to one of Paris' most prestigious locations.

There he launched a new design which included a beige trunk with red stripes, to immediate success with elite Parisians.

Perhaps the world's first luxury brand had been well and truly launched…

CHAPTER
TWO

AN UNPICKABLE
LOCK

IN 1890, LOUIS AND GEORGES
VUITTON LAUNCHED AN
INNOVATIVE LOCK SYSTEM TO
ENHANCE THE SECURITY OF THEIR
ICONIC TRUNKS.

TODAY, THE UNPICKABLE LOCK
REMAINS A HALLMARK OF THE
BRAND'S COMMITMENT TO
CRAFTMANSHIP AND QUALITY.

In 1871 Louis had sent his son Georges, then aged 14, to an English boarding school to get a better understanding of the language, with the ultimate goal being that Georges could deal with the many wealthy clients across the English Channel in future years.

"

The key selling point was that unlike all previous trunks, which were dome-shaped, Vuitton's trunks were rectangular – making them stackable and far more convenient for shipping via new means of transport like the railroad and steamship. Most commentators consider Vuitton's trunk the birth of modern luggage.

"

As quoted on Biography.com's Louis Vuitton feature , April 2021

Determined to expand the business beyond Paris and France, in 1885 Georges Vuitton opened the family's first premises in London.

He wanted to rival the best English luggage makers, though his initially overly French-themed store meant it would take five years – and a relocation to a better part of the city – to really establish the brand.

In 1890, Louis and Georges Vuitton revolutionized luggage locks with an ingenious closing system that turned travel trunks into real treasure chests.

Proudly claimed as "unpickable", it gave their designer luggage yet more appeal to those who could afford it.

Georges ensured the lock was patented to fend off copies and each came with a numbered key and serial number that was unique to the luggage it protected and allowed a set of luggage to be opened by the single key.

It was an inspired move and elevated Vuitton trunks to a global leader in their field.

The innovative lock design, being both secure as well as enabling customers to have their own unique keys, would set the standard for luggage around the world.

So confident were the Vuitton family that their unpickable lock was truly foolproof, that they invited world-famous escapologist Harry Houdini to attempt to prove them wrong – an offer he respectfully declined!

In 1889 Louis Vuitton won the coveted gold medal and the grand prize at the Exposition Universelle – a world fair held in Paris from the start of May to the end of October, which attracted more than 32 million visitors that year – for his brown and beige Damier design, which once again helped boost the popularity of the company's work.

Louis Vuitton passed away after losing his battle with brain cancer on 27 February 1892, aged 70, in Asnières-sur-Seine, France, leaving Georges to take sole control of the expanding business empire.

The continued success of the brand inevitably led to inferior copies and fakes being made, something Georges recognised and was determined to, at worst, minimize.

The trademark grey Trianon and the striped Rayée canvas in particular were targeted, so Georges created a chequerboard pattern of brown and beige squares with the Louis Vuitton registered trademark etched into the design.

It would, if anything, only further enhance the Vuitton range.

> "
>
> Old magazine adverts of Louis Vuitton products from the 1880's and 1890's warned the customer to 'Beware of Spurious Imitations!'. And so, in 1896, Georges introduced the famous Louis Vuitton monogram, making pieces much harder to imitate.
>
> "

TheRestory.com recalls the early issues Vuitton had to deal with in "The History of the Louis Vuitton Trunk"

CHAPTER
THREE

THE MONOGRAM CANVAS

IN 1896, THE ICONIC MONOGRAM CANVAS WAS LAUNCHED.

CREATED BY GEORGES VUITTON TO DETER IMITATORS, THE FAMOUS PRINT HAS BECOME SYNONYMOUS WITH THE BRAND, ADORNING A WIDE RANGE OF PRODUCTS, FROM HANDBAGS TO LUGGAGE.

After the death of his father, Georges Vuitton assumed sole responsibility for the management of the family business.

Georges was a very astute and innovative businessman. He travelled widely, including several trips to New York, and turned the company into a leading luxury destination worldwide.

Due to the rising popularity of the brand, many counterfeit products appeared in France. In a demand for authenticity, Georges created the Monogram Canvas.

This pattern would cover his trunks and reduce counterfeits due to the difficulty in recreating it. The pattern was first produced in 1896 and would later be copyrighted in 1902.

Georges' inspiration for the canvas is still unknown. Many believe that it is an homage to the Asian and Japanese aesthetics, while others believe he was inspired by the Gien's majolica tiles, decorated with four-petal flowers that were placed in the kitchen of his family's house in Asnières.

The monogram is made up of four different elements: three stylized floral motifs combined with the interlaced monogram of the company's founder.

One of the earliest symbols of modern luxury, it is the ideal combination of classic and modernity.

The first motif is a four-point star inside a diamond, which symbolizes passion. It is the ultimate symbol of union and passionate love.

THE MONOGRAM CANVAS

The second motif is a four-point star, symbolizing fortune.

Stars and flowers with four petals are notably seen in Egyptian art of the fourth century. They are seen as a fixed point in the universe guiding us to our destiny.

The third motif is a four-petal flower, which symbolizes joy. The flower sits inside a perfect circle, signifying protection and the absolute.

Like the Sun, the four-petal flower exudes a luminous aura of joy.

The motifs run parallel to the interlaced monogram, paying homage to Louis Vuitton.

The L and V are interlaced in such a way as to remain perfectly legible.

While the separate shapes are echoes of each other, the rigorous order in which they are placed creates the perfect pattern.

Over 100 years old, it is still a crucial part of the brand's identity and easily the most recognizable print from Louis Vuitton.

In 1996, the company celebrated the 100th anniversary of the iconic Monogram Canvas.

To mark the milestone, the company invited several designers from around the world to create their own unique pieces of luggage, bringing the brand's spirit of innovation and collaboration to fashion lovers across the globe.

The company needed a high-profile campaign to show the world they were modern and dynamic, so the designs of the seven – Azzedine Alaïa, Vivienne Westwood, Manolo Blahnik, Helmut Lang, Romeo Gigli, Sybilla and Isaac Mizrahi – were exhibited across the world.

The campaign gained lots of press attention and the items themselves became highly sought after by collectors. The company found itself presenting a new, fashionable face to the world of luxury luggage and used this as a steppingstone into the world of fashion design.

"

It's important to celebrate the monogram. It's the DNA of Vuitton. I think – I hope – there is an interest in the philosophy and culture of the Vuitton name. It's quite coherent and intellectual, and the products are great. These are things you will want to pass on – things you treasure.

"

Delphine Arnault

The executive vice-president of Louis Vuitton (from 2013), Delphine Arnault, on why the monogram means so much to the brand – as cited in the "Lunch with the FT" feature, Financial Times, *October 2014*

CHAPTER
FOUR

ESTABLISHING THE BRAND

LOUIS VUITTON'S SON, GEORGES, SUCCEEDED HIS FATHER AS HEAD OF THE BRAND, AND IN TIME, THAT HONOUR WENT TO GEORGES' SON GASTON-LOUIS.

THE PASSING OF THE BATON FROM FATHER TO SON ENSURED THE PERPETUATION OF THE BRAND'S DEDICATION TO EXCELLENCE AND INNOVATION.

The Louis Vuitton building, the largest travel-goods store in the world, was opened on the Champs-Élysées in 1914 and counted such luminaries as Coco Chanel as patrons.

> **"**
> Manufacturer of trunks, leather goods, goldsmith products and travel items, adorned with their most beautiful finery, become true works of art. **"**

Description of the business in the Louis Vuitton catalogue of 1914, as their luxury products range increased

In 1915, Coco Chanel commissioned Georges Vuitton to make her a bespoke handbag.

This would lead Louis Vuitton on an inaugural journey of smaller leather goods. So sought after and coveted was the Vuitton Chanel bag, that in the 1930s she gave permission for the bag to be enjoyed by others.

It was mass-produced (by Vuitton standards!) and, today, the Chanel handbag is known as the "Alma".

"

If you're trying to forge bonds on something other than kinship, and forge a tribal identity on something other than relatedness, conformity is a good way to do it. And if you're wealthy, you can do it with a very expensive It bag, or whether it's Vuitton or Valentino at the moment, and it's a way to signal to one another, *We're part of this tribe.*

"

Wednesday Martin

American author and cultural critic Wednesday Martin correctly suggests a Louis Vuitton handbag or travel bag is an exclusivity – a club, in effect. As quoted on Glamour.com

Just like his father had been, Georges was a natural innovator and visionary. He had predicted a boom in the automobile market and so designed luggage especially for the four-wheel mode of transport. But he didn't stop there, going as far as designing a car.

With the help of twin sons Jean and Pierre, they created what became known as a "voiturette".

The car was furnished with several of the Louis Vuitton automobile range items such as a wash-bowl, lunch set and a spare-parts trunk. Georges developed the idea further, creating what we would today recognize as one of the first camper vans in partnership with the Kellner coach-building company, which included rooftop sleeping berths, wash basin and a portable opening drinks bar! Genuis.

The Vuitton family weren't without tragedy, highlighted by Georges losing his twin sons within five years. Jean died in 1909, aged 10, after a short illness, and Pierre was 18 when he was killed fighting in the First World War.

That left Georges' eldest son, Gaston-Louis, as the sole heir to the family business.

66

The rainbow, a stretch of the imagination. In 1925, Gaston-Louis Vuitton wrote 'Let's turn the street into a cheerful space'. As select stores begin to re-open, hand-drawn rainbows by children and employees serve as welcoming beacons of hope during this uncertain time.

99

#LV

Tweet on official @LouisVuitton platform, 18 May 2020

The influence of Gaston-Louis Vuitton, Georges' eldest and only surviving son, grew steadily in the early decades of the 1900s. A legendary shop window designer for the flagship store at 70 Avenue des Champs-Élysées, he followed in a long line of Vuitton design innovators with his immaculate attention to detail. In 1927, he launched Maison Louis Vuitton's first perfume, named "Heures d'Absence", which was influenced by his love of travel and adventure.

Georges Vuitton passed away on 26 October 1936, aged 79.

As a result, Gaston-Louis became the head of Louis Vuitton and would give his three sons – Henry-Louis, Claude-Louis and Jacques-Louis – prominent roles within the business after the liberation of Paris in 1944.

CHAPTER
FIVE

VUITTON:
THE GO-TO BRAND

FROM RED-CARPET EVENTS TO
ELITE GATHERINGS,
LOUIS VUITTON'S HANDBAGS,
CLOTHING AND ACCESSORIES
HAVE BECOME COVETED
SYMBOLS OF AFFLUENCE AND
SOPHISTICATION.

THE BRAND'S ABILITY TO
CONSISTENTLY DELIVER OPULENCE
AND TIMELESS ELEGANCE
CEMENTS ITS POSITION AS THE
ULTIMATE CHOICE FOR THE
RICH AND FAMOUS.

Attracting the great and good as unwitting ambassadors of your label has always been the major goal of any fashionable organization – and Louis Vuitton was no different. From the 1920s onwards, many rich and famous artists favoured the Art Deco trunks and luggage created by Gaston-Louis Vuitton – including writer F. Scott Fitzgerald and wife Zelda, Ernest Hemingway and Pablo Picasso.

Bag shapes that remain popular fashion staples today were introduced throughout the 1900s. The Steamer bag, a smaller piece designed to be kept inside the luggage trunks, was introduced in 1901. The Keepall bag was debuted in 1930, followed by the Noé bag, which was originally designed to carry Champagne, in 1932, and, in 1966, the cylindrical Papillon bag.

"

Thanks to their instantly recognisable monogram, Louis Vuitton bags are among the most in demand both in the new and resale markets and, with its timeless duffel silhouette, the Speedy Keepall is one of the brand's best sellers. Available new in sizes from 25–40cm, the Speedy debuted in the

1930s as a design for travellers and has been the subject of countless limited editions and collaborative versions. It is also one of the most popular Louis Vuitton bags to get personalised.

"

As quoted on HauteHistory.com's "A Brief History of the 'It' bag"

The Keepall bag would become one of the world's most durable – and iconic – pieces of luggage, designed and introduced by Gaston-Louis Vuitton as a moderately sized weekend bag – ideal for short trips or weekends away. It encapsulated the shifting landscape of the casual traveller in that it is light, flexible and, of course, highly desirable.

The 1950s arguably put Louis Vuitton at the top of the tree for must-have handbags and travel luggage.

French cinema's "New Wave" caused a surge in popularity – particularly in the Saint-Tropez area of the French Riviera – where film stars were continually followed by the word's paparazzi.

Towards the start of the 1960s, "New Wave" captured the imagination of the world thanks to the vision and creativity of a group of maverick directors.

The emergence of Brigitte Bardot, arguably the face of New Wave, proved a vital part of the Louis Vuitton evolution, with Bardot – a huge fan of the soft-side Keepall – rarely without Vuitton travel accessories.

Thanks to advances in technology and a new coating process, a supple version of the Monogram Canvas was created in 1959, which meant it could now be used for purses, bags and wallets.

"

Louis Vuitton has been long regarded as one of the world's most recognizable status symbols, and as such, it has often adorned stars on the silver screen to show just how rich and powerful their character is.

"

As cited in Weekly Lux Drop by Maria Itosu, April 2021

At the height of her fame in the late 1950s and early 1960s and the epitome of chic and timeless style, *Breakfast at Tiffany's* star Audrey Hepburn was often seen carrying the popular "Speedy" travel bag.

The "Speedy 25" – often described as "the perfect city holdall" – was designed at Audrey Hepburn's request for a smaller, more portable version of her favourite piece of luggage. It has since proved one of the most popular and iconic of all Vuitton bags.

If Brigitte Bardot had helped elevate Louis Vuitton back to the top of the uber-cool accessories tree, the following decade would see the brand positively rocket as two of the most idolised women on the planet – the Vuitton-loving Audrey Hepburn and President John F. Kennedy's style guru wife Jackie – were never seen without a desirable Louis Vuitton item of one sort or another. It was literally money-can't-buy advertising which was essentially without cost.

Gaston-Louis Vuitton died in 1970. A shrewd businessman, just like his grandfather Louis and father Georges, he had successfully steered the family business through the Second World War and ensured the path through the 1950s and 1960s was one that once again saw the brand associated with the fashionistas as well as the aspirational.

A design genius, he influenced a generation and ensured Louis Vuitton continually moved forward.

With no natural heir to the Louis Vuitton throne following Gaston-Louis' death, the business continued to be profitable, but ambled along rather than powering forward under an innovative leader with the Vuitton DNA.

In 1977, Gaston-Louis' children and their spouses discussed the way forward – and in the end manufacturing mogul Henry Racamier – husband of Gaston-Louis' daughter Odile – became company president.

His first task was to increase the global reach of LV, and by the mid-1980s, Henry Racamier's grand extension plans for Louis Vuitton gathered momentum as he bought controlling interests in other luxury brands, including Givenchy, Loewe, and revered champagne producer Veuve Clicquot.

In 1987, Henry Racamier oversaw the merger with one of the world's largest and most prestigious champagne producers, Moët Hennessy – thus creating the luxury mega-brand that is LVMH (Moët Hennessy Louis Vuitton).

It was one of the world's most famous mergers, valued at $4 billion!

A sale? No!

Henry Racamier

The LV president reacts to a reporter's question as to whether he'd ever considered having a sale at his stores! As cited in Henry Racamier's obituary in The Economist, *April 2003*

Henry Racamier's decision to recruit French business magnate Bernard Arnault during the LVMH merger would backfire, however, and after three years of legal wrangling, Arnault – backed by various huge investors – gained control of LVMH and promptly ejected Racamier from the board. Bernard Arnault took over the running of LVMH on 13 January 1989.

In 1996, after a period of relatively poor sales, Louis Vuitton needed a new direction.

The brand had lost its aura of exclusivity and luxury somewhat, and so the decision was made to redesign the iconic Damier canvas for a new line of luggage and celebrate a century of the iconic monogram motif.

CHAPTER
SIX

THE
MARC JACOBS
ERA

THE APPOINTMENT OF MARC
JACOBS AS ARTISTIC DIRECTOR IN
1997 USHERED IN A NEW ERA FOR
THE FASHION HOUSE.

INFUSING THE BRAND WITH
HIS UNIQUE VISION, THE
DESIGNER EMBRACED A FUSION
OF HIGH FASHION AND STREET
STYLE, CAPTIVATING A YOUNGER,
EDGIER AUDIENCE.

In 1997, with a new vision for the company, LVMH CEO Arnault took the decision to bring in maverick but highly regarded American designer Marc Jacobs as Louis Vuitton's new creative director.

Jacobs had created his own label and was seen as the man to help change the direction and perception of the brand.

"

It's very important that when you have a designer like Marc Jacobs, who is a genius, you give him complete freedom.

"

Bernard Arnault

"

We couldn't make it look like old Vuitton, because there was no tradition… So I started from zero, without putting an insignia on the outside of things – just in the linings, pieces in pale grey like the original Vuitton trunks and in fabric like bonded cotton that had both luxury and practicality.

"

Marc Jacobs

Jacobs talks about his debut Louis Vuitton collection, March 1998

"

It took five hours in an off-road vehicle to reach the location, which is the largest impact crater in Chile. When I got there the sun was going down and I didn't have time to put a camera stand, I threw a sandbag on the ground, balanced my camera on it, I took two photos with two different rockets.

"

Jean Larivière

Celebrated Louis Vuitton photographer Jean Larivière reveals some of the lengths he went to to get the perfect shot for the brand's various advertising campaigns

"

We just worked with shapes. Darts, folds, and pleats. I don't like to use these words because they sound pretentious, but if you like, last season was painterly, and this season's sculptural.

"

Marc Jacobs

Jacobs comments on the Louis Vuitton autumn/winter collection of 2008

"

Clothes mean nothing until someone lives in them.

Marc Jacobs

Jacobs reiterates his desire to create fashion that is useable rather than catwalk one-offs – as cited in Glamour's "26 of the most memorable quotes that prove fashion is so much more than frivolity", January 2021

"

What made Louis Vuitton famous was the quality. We don't do marketing; we just create products which are exceptional in their design and craftsmanship.

"

Bernard Arnault

Each and every Louis Vuitton handbag is handmade and takes about a week to create.

Louis Vuitton handbags are never discounted.

"

I love to take things that are everyday and make them into the most luxurious things in the world.

"

Marc Jacobs

The driving force behind Louis Vuitton and the challenges he sets himself – as cited in Marie Claire's "16 Marc Jacobs Quotes That Prove He Is the Wisest of Fashion Gods", April 2015

"

Marc had seen a few pictures of me in sunglasses. He wanted to know what my take on sunglasses would be like for Louis Vuitton. He pretty much let me go into my own world. I thought that was great.

"

Pharrell Williams

As quoted in Women's Wear Daily, *October 2004*

"

When I took over Louis Vuitton, everyone said, 'It's already so big – what more can you do?' And since then, we've multiplied that success tenfold.

"

Bernard Arnault

"

Fashion is about dressing according to what's fashionable. Style is more about being yourself.

"

Marc Jacobs

"

It's a multidimensional brand.
The trunk maker was first created
around the world of travel, then
around the art of living. It is now
developed in all segments, and
each time it diversifies, it makes
a point of being the best in
everything.

"

Yves Hanania

*The founder of the consultancy firm Lighthouse and co-author
of the book Le luxe contre-attaque, accélérations et disruptions,
celebrates LVMH's diversity and innovation.*

"

I don't think there is just one Louis Vuitton woman. That is why, for the fall/winter 2011 show, I loved the idea of lots of different characters – a wife, a mistress, a girlfriend – stepping out of the row of hotel elevators.

Marc Jacobs

explains the thinking behind his autumn/winter collection, 2011

"

I don't want to sound too silly or pretentious about this, but, you know, I love being in Paris. I love working at Louis Vuitton. I love fashion. That's why I do it. No one's forcing me to do this. And nobody forces anyone to buy it. It's a real love affair.

"

Marc Jacobs

66

It was never my desire to revolutionize fashion, to make clothes that could be in a museum. I want to create clothes that have a certain style, but I want to see them used.

99

Marc Jacobs

Making clothes that are useable rather than impractical underpins all Jacobs' work – as cited in Marie Claire's "16 Marc Jacobs Quotes That Prove He Is the Wisest of Fashion Gods", April 2015

66

Louis Vuitton, the world's biggest luxury brand in terms of sales, is planning to dampen its expansion worldwide and focus on high-end products to preserve its exclusive image.

99

Bernard Arnault

Louis Vuitton chief Bernard Arnault suggests less is more, as quoted on Fashion Network, 2013

"

The fash pack gave a standing ovation when Marc Jacobs presented his last-ever collection for Louis Vuitton. The designer reworked props from his greatest hit sets, but this time the carousel, the escalators and the station clock all came coated in black lacquer. To finish, he gave us a finale of black feather headdresses, dedicated to 'the showgirl in all of us.' Now that's what we call an exit.

"

As cited in Marie Claire's "10 Most Memorable Louis Vuitton Fashion Show Moments Ever" by Caroline Leaper, August 2016

66

As far back as I can remember, I had an interest in fashion. I used to go to sleep-away camp, and they'd provide a list of things that you had to bring, and I always wanted to be a bit more creative than the list allowed. Like, if they required chinos, I wanted to hand-paint them.

99

Marc Jacobs

Jacobs reveals he was pushing the boundaries from an early age – as cited in Marie Claire's "16 Marc Jacobs Quotes That Prove He Is the Wisest of Fashion Gods", April 2015

"

The first time at Louis Vuitton
was spring 2009 season, and I
remember that the colours of the
clothes were very dreamy.

"

Liu Wen

*Chinese supermodel Liu Wen recalls her first experience with
Louis Vuitton*

66

Marc Jacobs is full of creative people and Louis Vuitton is again a name on the door, a name that has existed for many years, but I'm a collaborator there and I bring in other people, other artists, and I work with a great creative design team.

99

Marc Jacobs

Marc Jacobs perhaps underplays his role at LVMH...

"

I'm not really rebellious, but it was kind of a clever solution to doing what we were told by a certain old guard at Louis Vuitton we couldn't do: 'You don't deface the Monogram; you don't change the Monogram.' There was a certain respect and a disrespect (in scribbling on the Monogram). Again if anything we only amplified the attention to the Monogram by writing on top of it.

"

Marc Jacobs

Marc Jacobs describes the thinking behind the hugely successful Louis Vuitton graffiti bags, 2012

Campaigns

Louis Vuitton cultivated a strong celebrity following under Jacobs' direction, with many models, actors and musicians acting as the face of the brand. In 2007, the Core Values campaign was aimed at showcasing Louis Vuitton's travel roots, and celebrities such as Angelina Jolie, Bono, Sean Connery, Keith Richards and Catherine Deneuve appeared as part of the project.

Other campaigns have included Natalia Vodianova, Christy Turlington and Kate Elson for autumn/winter 2010–11. Madonna appeared for spring/summer 2009, while Diane Kruger, Chloe Sevigny, Christina Ricci and Scarlett Johansson were immersed in the spring/summer 2007. Scarlett Johansson had also been involved in the autumn/winter collection of 2004–05 and Jennifer Lopez for autumn/winter 2003–04.

Marc Jacobs would enjoy collaborations with young, upcoming artists and designers.

Takashi Murakami was one such example and Louis Vuitton collaborated with him from 2002 to 2015 and incorporated many of Murakami's influences, which were inspired by traditional Japanese art, anime and manga, sci-fi and pop culture.

"

The Louis Vuitton woman is more about a quality – a quality within some women that needs to come forward, to be noticed and recognized.

"

Marc Jacobs

"

I always find beauty in things that are odd and imperfect. They are much more interesting.

"

Marc Jacobs

Jacobs lends an insight into his unique thinking on fashion – as cited in Vogue's "51 Best Fashion Quotes", 2020

After every season, if any of Louis Vuitton's products are not sold, then they are sent back to its factory in France and shredded or burned, in order to sustain an item's value and class of brand.

"

When you see a fashion show, you see those seven minutes of what was six months of tedious work. Going up an inch and down an inch, changing it from one shade of red to another shade of red.

"

Marc Jacobs

Marc Jacobs, as cited in Marie Claire's "16 Marc Jacobs Quotes That Prove He Is the Wisest of Fashion Gods" by Caroline Leaper, 2015

66

What I have in mind are things that are deluxe but that you can also throw into a bag and escape town with, because Louis Vuitton has a heritage in travel.

99

Marc Jacobs

"

To the showgirl in all of us.

"

Marc Jacobs

Marc signs off his final Louis Vuitton collection in the spring/summer of 2014

In October 2013, Marc Jacobs stepped down as Louis Vuitton's Creative Director to focus on his own label.

Jacobs was at the helm for 16 years and helped the brand grow to unprecedented levels during his hugely successful and innovative tenure.

CHAPTER
SEVEN

PUSHING THE ENVELOPE

THE APPOINTMENT OF NICHOLAS GHESQUIÈRE AS ARTISTIC DIRECTOR IN 2013 MARKED ANOTHER MILESTONE IN THE BRAND'S EVOLUTION.

JOINING FROM THE MORE EXPERIMENTAL BALENCIAGA, GHESQUIÈRE SET ABOUT MODERNIZING THE ESTABLISHED LOUIS VUITTON AESTHETIC.

A New Direction

Marc Jacobs' successor at Louis Vuitton would be Nicolas Ghesquière, who became the new artistic director in November 2013.

After taking an unorthodox route into fashion design that had some echoes of Louis Vuitton's own journey to greatness, Ghesquière had steadily risen in the industry.

He had transformed the fortunes of Balenciaga (owned by LVMH's main competitor, Kering), and created the celebrated "Lariat" bag, also known as the "Motorcycle" bag – which brought him to the attention of LVMH chief Bernard Arnault.

"

He is a brilliant designer and he'll do something completely different … I've always admired Nicolas. I'm curious to see what he'll do.

"

Marc Jacobs

endorses the appointment of Nicolas Ghesquière as his successor, 2013

"

I'm really glad someone I respect and admire, and think is a really great talent, is there.

"

Marc Jacobs

endorses the appointment of Nicolas Ghesquière as his successor, 2013

"

…whose legacy I wholeheartedly
hope to honour.

"

Nicolas Ghesquière

pays homage to departing LVMH supremo Marc Jacobs

66

What you think of as normal, and classic, was once new.

99

Nicolas Ghesquière

"

When I went to my first Paris Fashion Week, I had been invited to the Louis Vuitton show by Nicolas. We met there. It was all organic and fun for me.

"

Selena Gomez

Selena Gomez reflects on her first meeting with Nicolas Ghesquière, as quoted on TooFab.com

"

Today is a new day. A big day.
Words cannot express exactly how
I am feeling at this moment…
Above all, immense joy.

"

Nicolas Ghesquière

Nicolas Ghesquière's typewritten note placed on the seats of everyone attending the closing spot of Paris Fashion Week for the 2014 Louis Vuitton autumn/winter collection

"

I have a passion for modern and contemporary art. I spend a lot of time in museums; I particularly like the Guggenheim, MoMA in New York or LACMA and the Getty Museum in Los Angeles, for example. I cannot wait for the Louis Vuitton Foundation to open.

"

Delphine Arnault

Executive Vice President of LVMH can't hide her excitement at the opening of the Louis Vuitton Foundation, as quoted on LoveExpands.com, 2014

"

I didn't explore that much yet
the sophistication and the more
dressed-up part of Louis Vuitton.

"

Nicolas Ghesquière

*Nicolas Ghesquière comments on his spring/summer 2017
show collection*

"

My question this season was less about one theme; it was about this zone between femininity and masculinity. This zone is highlighted by non-binary people, people that are taking a lot of freedom dressing themselves as they want, and, in turn, giving a lot of freedom to all of us.

"

Nicolas Ghesquière

"

Louis Vuitton is the most visible, the most showy, in a way. Some people think it's terrible, some people love it, some people just have a fascination with it.

"

Nicolas Ghesquière

"

What does eccentricity mean today?

"

Nicolas Ghesquière

The Louis Vuitton artistic director refers to the work of friend Coddington, who designed a quirky range of handbags for the brand – as cited in British Vogue's "Louis Vuitton: Art and Craft on the French Riviera" by Suzie Menkes, May 2018

> **"**
> I don't put cash in my Louis Vuitton wallet. I have it thrown around my bag – just a whole bunch of hundreds, maybe $5,000. **"**

Nicki Minaj

Singer/songwriter Nicki Minaj reveals her "pocket money" cash habits! As quoted on Millyuns.com

"

You always have to fight with gravity when you design clothes. You want the clothes to be suspended in space or to move with the woman wearing them, and I think that's interesting – the relationship with movement, like works of art.

"

Nicolas Ghesquière

Ghesquière muses on his inspirations and vision – as cited in British Vogue's *"Louis Vuitton: Art and Craft on the French Riviera" by Suzie Menkes, May 2018*

"

Why would I want to do my own label when I can do fantastic things here [at Louis Vuitton] and put my spin on things?

"

Kim Jones

The LVMH artistic director 2011–2018 speaking in 2013, as cited in French Vogue, March 2018

"

I remember the first Louis Vuitton bag I received: it was a brown Noé bag, when I was 18. You are still very privileged to receive a Louis Vuitton bag for your 18th birthday.

"

Delphine Arnault

The Executive Vice President of Louis Vuitton recalls a gift she has never forgotten – as quoted in "Lunch with the FT", Financial Times, October 2014

> "
> The reason I collaborate with Louis Vuitton is that Louis Vuitton is number one in the world, and I am honoured to work with them.
> "

Yayoi Kusama

Japanese contemporary artist Yayoi Kusama on her collaboration with Louis Vuitton, as quoted on RewindVintage.co.uk

66

As a designer, the things you can do at Vuitton are second to none. In LVMH, they are very respectful of the designer, you are a special person in the company. You can't be that naive about the world, you have to get on with stuff.

99

Kim Jones

The LVMH artistic director 2011–2018 speaking in 2013 as cited in French Vogue, March 2018

LVMH-owned Louis Vuitton is the world's largest luxury house: its sales surged 20 per cent to €20.6 billion in 2022 and are expected to reach €21.9 billion in 2023.

CHAPTER

EIGHT

THE MAVERICKS

WITH THE HIRING OF THE
MUCH-ADMIRED VIRGIL ABLOH
IN 2018, THE BRAND LOOKED TO
A MAVERICK GENERATION OF
BRILLIANT DESIGNERS TO MOVE
INTO A MORE DIVERSE AND
ECLECTIC DIRECTION.

THE FUTURE OF LOUIS VUITTON
HAS NEVER LOOKED MORE
EXCITING...

In 2018, brilliant designer Virgil Abloh – creator of the hugely successful Off-White label – was appointed as head of menswear design at Louis Vuitton, becoming the first black designer at the fashion house and the most visible black designer in fashion.

66

Don't underestimate the cosmetic power of sunglasses. It's worth spending a bit of money on a quality pair. I usually go for Dior or Louis Vuitton.

99

Dita Von Teese

American dancer, model and businesswoman Dita Von Teese on the merits of expensive shades!

"

This opportunity to think through what the next chapter of design and luxury will mean at a brand that represents the pinnacle of luxury was always a goal in my wildest dreams. And to show a younger generation that there is no one way anyone in this kind of position has to look is a fantastically modern spirit in which to start. **"**

Virgil Abloh

Louis Vuitton's new head of menswear design, as cited in the New York Times, *March 2018*

"

There's a lot of baggage that
comes along with our family, but
it's like Louis Vuitton baggage.

"

Kim Kardashian

American socialite Kim Kardashian's classic quote suggesting her
family have stylish, high-end issues! As quoted from the TV series,
Keeping Up With the Kardashians

"

My muse has always been what people actually wear, and I am really excited to make a luxury version of that.

"

Virgil Abloh

New York Times, *March 2018*

"

Hey! You know what happens to a snake when a Louis Vuitton heel steps on it? Shut the hell up, or you'll find out!

"

Veronica Lodge

A classic line from the sharp-tongued cult status animated character Veronica Lodge. As quoted on Magical Quote

"

I got to be a lot more thoughtful about man's relationship to Earth. I decided there's so much placed on 'the new' in fashion. I'm saying to my consumer that value doesn't deteriorate over time.

"

Virgil Abloh

The maverick designer on his spring/summer 2021 collection as cited in Vogue, January 2021

> **"**
>
> I love counterfeits, it's the best feedback. It's better than a great review in *Vogue*. If it's working to a point where someone else can profit… it's really working.
>
> **"**

Virgil Abloh

Imitation is indeed the greatest form of flattery according to Abloh – as quoted on TheArtGorgeous.com's "Inspiring Virgil Abloh Quotes", December 2021

"

Look at your eyes. You've got
bigger bags than Louis Vuitton.

"

Matt Dunn

The Ex-Boyfriend's Handbook, *October 2006*

"

Fashion is one of the greatest vehicles to merge music, art, architecture, design, typography — it's a wide enough canvas, or a big enough sandbox, to touch all the different things that I'm into.

"

Virgil Abloh

66

I feel like I'm figuring things out, but I don't feel accomplished yet. I still feel like I'm an intern.

99

Virgil Abloh

Abloh's typically self-depreciative opinion of his work, as quoted on Dazed.com, November 2021

"

My first big career purchase when I was, like, 17 was a Louis Vuitton laptop bag. Now, seeing the exhibit (Louis Vuitton's 'Series 3' exhibition in London), it's exciting because I feel like I kind of know it. It's weird – it's almost like something you grow up with and you just know a little bit about it. Now that I'm immersed in it, it's kind of insane.

"

Selena Gomez

American singer and actress Selena Gomez on her long association with Louis Vuitton. As quoted on TooFab.com, June 2016

"

The one thing that I think the luxury market needs to understand is that culture has changed. I don't know if there's any way to underline that any further. This should be in bold writing – that luxury by a 17-year-old's standard is completely different than his parents'. His version of luxury is streetwear.

"

Virgil Abloh

66

A 17-year-old can be more advanced and often is more advanced than a 45-year-old, so my design theory and the culture that surrounds Off-White is non-traditional.

99

Virgil Abloh

as quoted on WWD.com's "Virgil Abloh most memorable quotes"

All Louis Vuitton bags are waterproof and fireproof – one of the reasons why they are so expensive.

"

Abloh is the fulcrum point of these changing times in fashion, creating common ground between the aesthetics of the cultures of streetwear and the exclusive domain of luxury.

"

Sarah Mower

comments on Virgil Abloh's spring/summer collection, as cited in Vogue, *2020*

66

You know who I am most inspired by? That kid that hasn't had the chance to showcase their brand yet. Those kids motivate the work I do every day. That's the muse for me: the next generation. And I want my work to inspire people like them.

99

Virgil Abloh

Virgil Abloh, speaking in 2016, as quoted on Dazed.com by Rahel Aklilu, November 2021

"

Imagine if I really believed I was taking 'fashion' and turning it on its head. That to me is easy. You can be a disruptor, but it doesn't mean you're any good. All I'm trying to do is create things that are indicative of my surroundings and the community that I come from, so that more people can do them.

"

Virgil Abloh

Abloh explains his drive and vision, as quoted on Dazed.com, November 2021

"

My power is to show Black talent, Black people, and Black people inside of my output.

"

Virgil Abloh

As cited in British Vogue, "From the Archive" by Olivia Singer, November 2021

Not only was she the face of Louis Vuitton in 2009, but Madonna even has a bag named after her.

The summer of that year LV released the Ltd. Kalahari Madonna GM Bag, additionally named after the famous Kalahari desert in sub-Saharan Africa.

"

Someone said [my appointment at Louis Vuitton] felt like [Barack] Obama getting elected president – like the same epiphany. We got that it was possible, but we didn't think [it would happen]. When it's official, it's different.

"

Virgil Abloh

"

The idea is to find chicness. I think there's an absolute beauty that exists within every moment in culture, and so I'm trying to make things that are youthful, timely and timeless, but in a quality that's surprising.

"

Virgil Abloh

> 66
>
> Life is so short you can't waste even a day subscribing to what someone thinks you can do versus knowing what you can do.
>
> 99

Virgil Abloh

Abloh's prophetic and sound advice, as quoted on Dazed.com, November 2021

On 21 November 2021, Virgil Abloh passed away aged only 41. His family announced his death on Instagram. "For over two years, Virgil valiantly battled a rare, aggressive form of cancer, cardiac angiosarcoma. He chose to endure his battle privately since his diagnosis in 2019, undergoing numerous challenging treatments, all while helming several significant institutions that span fashion, art, and culture."

"

Not only a genius designer, a visionary, he was also a man with a beautiful soul and great wisdom.

"

Bernard Arnault

The LVMH chairman and chief executive pays his respects to Virgil Abloh after his untimely passing, as cited in British Vogue, November 2021

"

Forever adored, forever magical.

"

Gigi Hadid

Gigi Hadid, supermodel and regular collaborator with Virgil Abloh, pays her respects on her official Instagram page, 2021

"

You're probably redesigning the gates of Heaven right now. I'm praying for your family. Rest in Power King.

Amina Muaddi

Supermodel Amina Muaddi posts a tribute to Virgil Abloh, as cited on @aminamuaddi official Instagram page, November 2021

"

Through it all, his work ethic, infinite curiosity, and optimism never wavered. Virgil was driven by his dedication to his craft and to his mission to open doors for others and create pathways for greater equality in art and design. He often said, 'Everything I do is for the 17-year-old version of myself,' believing deeply in the power of art to inspire future generations.

"

Statement on Virgil Abloh's official Instagram page after his untimely death, as cited on The Guardian, *November 2021*

According to estimates in 2022, the label's sales will be close to €22 billion, while its operating profit (Ebit) will rise to more than €10 billion in 2022 with a margin close to 50%. Today, it has 33,000 employees worldwide and plans to recruit 9,000 new staff within three years. It has 460 shops in around 60 countries, including France, South Korea, Japan and the United States. As for production, it relies on 19 workshops in France and three sites in Italy, including a shoe factory.

> **"** Louis Vuitton indicates a lively family life, albeit with plenty of style. **"**

Quote source unknown, as cited on thefamouspeople.com

> **"**
>
> Pharrell Williams is a visionary whose creative universes expand from music to art, and to fashion. The way in which he breaks boundaries across the various worlds he explores aligns with Louis Vuitton's status as a cultural maison, reinforcing its values of innovation, pioneer spirit and entrepreneurship.
>
> **"**

LVMH statement confirms musician, producer and fashion icon Pharrell Williams is the fashion house's new artistic director, as cited in The Guardian, *February 2023*

"

I am glad to welcome Pharrell back home, after our collaborations in 2004 and 2008 for Louis Vuitton, as our new Men's Creative Director. His creative vision beyond fashion will undoubtedly lead Louis Vuitton towards a new and very exciting chapter.

"

Pietro Beccari

Pietro Beccari's first big move as the new Louis Vuitton Chairman and CEO is to appoint musician, rapper, record producer and fashion designer Pharrell Williams. As quoted in Harper's Bazaar, February 2023

"

You have to understand, I am just a regular dude. At the end of the day, this is all an incredible dream come true. He is Marc Jacobs, and it is Louis Vuitton, and who am I for that matter?

"

Pharrell Williams

Pharrell Williams after his 2004 collaboration with Louis Vuitton to produce sunglasses, as quoted in British Vogue, 2014

"

Is that weird, taking my Louis Vuitton bag camping?

"

Jessica Simpson

The American actress and singer raises a moot point ahead of her camping expedition, as quoted on Quotes.net

"

The mission of the LVMH group is to represent the most refined qualities of Western 'Art de Vivre' around the world. LVMH must continue to be synonymous with both elegance and creativity. Our products, and the cultural values they embody, blend tradition and innovation, and kindle dream and fantasy.

"

LVMH Mission Statement, 2023

66

There's a fear, it's like a creative thing, like you might miss the next idea by just not being in the right place at the right time or being open to seeing the trends evolve. Culture moves at a crazy pace.

99

Virgil Abloh

"

I like to get one pair of shoes and wear them till they're dirty. Besides, I don't walk – I glide, like butter. Float like a vampire. I'm like Louis Vuitton, but smoother. He wishes he were like me.

"

Kid Cudi

American rapper, songwriter and producer Kid Cudi can't hide the high esteem he holds himself in! As quoted on AZQuotes.com, "Best Louis Vuitton Quotes"

"

My mom used to work for Coach and Louis Vuitton, in retail. So, I've always been around it. I've always had that connection. Always.

"

Travis Scott

American rapper, singer, songwriter and record producer Scott on his maternally influenced fashion preferences. As quoted on quotlr.com's "30 Charming Quotes on Vuitton"

"

It is a creative cultural company that reaches a very large customer base, from the youngest, with Gen Z, to more mature customers. A culture brand with a global audience, something completely different to what you see in fashion.

"

Bernard Arnault

The LVMH CEO spells out what the brand really means, as quoted on Fashion Network, 14 February 2023